A Whales Tail, Eh

By

Lizy J Campbell

A Whales Tail, Eh

A Mostly Ontario Canada Themed Poetry Book

Content

Cherry Beach Love

Market of Culture

Thousand Island Bliss

EH!

I Don't Live in an Igloo, eh!

The Six

The Dome of Hopes

A Whales Tail, Yum

Oh Henry, Thank you

Caribana Delight

Let The Jazz Play

Canadas Wonderland

The Mighty Waterfall

Muskoka Tranquility

The Hill

Canada, eh

Oh Canada, land of mountains high

Where the lakes glisten and geese fly

From coast to coast, our country stretches wide

With diversity in every tide

From the rocky shores of Newfoundland and
Labrador

To the rugged peaks of British Columbia

We are proud of our land

We are hockey players and maple leaf flag
wavers who cheer!

Timbits lovers and poutine cravers

We are strong and free, as our anthem sings
our hearts fill with pride

We are multicultural and bilingual

A melting pot of people, all unique and special

We stand together,

A nation, strong and grand

Oh Canada, our home and native land

We'll defend you with our heart, with our bare
hands

We'll sing of your beauty, everywhere

We are Canadians

Sorry

Canadian winter life

The snow falls softly, blanketing the land

A winter wonderland, so pure and grand

A blanket of white, as far as the eye can see

A Canadian winter, so serene and free

The trees bow low, under the weight of snow

A winter landscape, a natural show

Icicles glisten, on rooftops so high

A winter's morning, a clear blue sky

Skaters glide on these frozen ponds

Children laugh, as they make snowmen in the yard

The smell of woodsmoke, in the crisp air

A Canadian winter, so picturesque and fair

The snow falls harder, as night draws near

A silent world, so peaceful and dear

A land of snow and ice, so wild and vast

A Canadian winter, forever it feels to last

Where winter brings, a snowy wonderland

We embrace it all though, this cold and chill

For in our hearts, a love for winter will forever
thrill

Lake Ontario

Lake Ontario, vast and blue
A body of water, so grand and true

From the Niagara Falls to the Thousand Islands

Your beauty is unmatched, your splendor
shines

The waves crashing on the shore

A symphony of sound, forever more

The breeze blowing through the trees

A refreshing touch, a natural ease

Fishing boats bob on the waves

As the seagull's call, it's nature's symphonic
craves

The sun setting over the horizon

A breathtaking view, a true realization

The cities that line your shores Toronto,
Kingston, and more

Each with their own unique charm

A reflection of your natural calm

Lake Ontario, you are a treasure

A symbol of Canada's natural pleasure

We cherish the memories we make

On your shores and the life, you shape

So, here's to you, Lake Ontario

Our admiration for you

Poutine

Fries, gravy, and cheese curds piled high

A Canadian delicacy, a true guilty pleasure, no
lie

A dish that warms the heart and soul

Poutine, you have a special hold

Crispy fries, golden and hot

Smothered in gravy, a savory pot

Topped with cheese curds, oh so squeaky

A taste sensation, that's truly unique-y

From the streets of Quebec to the far north

Poutine can be found, in every corner

A staple at fairs and truck stops too

A dish that brings people together, it's good

Some like it spicy, some like it loaded

No matter the way, it's always devoured

Poutine, you are a Canadian treasure

A dish we can't get enough, now and forever

So, here's to you, poutine, our guilty pleasure

A dish that brings us together

Maple Sweet

Maple, sweet and pure

A symbol of Canada, forever allure

From the tree to the syrup, we pour

Your essence is an integral part of our culture

In the Spring, the sap begins to flow

A sign of renewal, a natural show

The tapping of the trees, a tradition old

A process that's been passed down, stories told

The boiling down of sap, a labor of love

A sweet aroma, that's sent from above

The syrup collects, in jugs so warm

A taste of Canada, in every form

From pancakes to ice cream, maple's there

A flavor that's uniquely Canadian, beyond
compare

In Fall, the leaves turn, a sight to behold

A natural wonder, that's worth the wait to be
told

Maple, you are a treasure, a taste divine

A symbol of Canada, entwined

In our hearts and souls, you'll always be

A part of our culture, a beautiful tree

CN Tower

The CN Tower, tall and proud

A beacon of Canada, a symbol unbound

Rising high above the city's skyline

A remarkable sight, so grand so fine

A structure of steel, a marvel of design

A testament to human ingenuity, that's the six

The elevator ride, so fast

A view of the city, a sight that will last

The Edge Walk, a thrill

A walk around the tower, with a view like no other

The city below, a sprawling sight

A view that takes our breath away

From the tower's top, the world is small

A perspective that's unique, to see it all

The tower stands, a symbol of might

A Canadian icon, a delight

The CN Tower

A remarkable sight

A beacon of hope

A symbol of strength

A reflection of our nation's pride

Torono

Toronto, a city of contrasts

A mix of old and new, a city that enchants

From the CN Tower to the lakefront shore

A city with so much to explore

The streets are alive, with the hustle

A vibrant energy, that's truly a bustle

From the trendy neighborhoods to the historic sites

Toronto has it all

The CN tower, a landmark to see

The Kensington market, a melting pot of culture

A place to explore, with so many flavors

The Toronto Islands, an escape from the city's pace

A place to relax, and enjoy nature's grace

Toronto, a city of diversity

A melting pot of cultures, with so much variety

A city that embraces all, with open arms

Canadian Geese

Canadian geese, in V-formation fly

A sight to see, as they grace the sky

Their honking calls, a melody not so sweet

A herald of spring, a sign to go outside

Majestic birds, with wings spread wide

Their journey well, they weren't missed here

A symbol of Canada, but don't get too close

From the North they fly, to warmer climes

Their migration, a journey

A symbol of determination, and grace

Canadian geese, a true wonder to trace

In the fall, they return to their home

Their honking calls, a familiar tone

Canadian geese, the bully of birds

These Canadian geese, are wild and free

A sight to see, in skies so blue and clear

A bird that all Canadians fear

(You thought I was going to say something bad about them, huh? Yeah, I don't want it pooping on my lawn or attacking me so, let's just leave it at that)

Snowmobiler Thrill

The snow falls, a blanket of white

A winter wonderland

The sound of a motor, in the distance heard

A snowmobiler, on a journey, embarked

Across the trails, with speed and grace

A rush of wind, a smile on their face

The snowflakes dance, in the headlights' beam

A winter adventure, like a dream

The crisp air, a refreshing breeze

Nature's beauty, in winter freeze

Through the forests, and over the hills

A snowmobiler's thrill, their hearts fill

The journey, a true test of skill

With the snow and the cold, a true thrill

The snowmobiling, a Canadian pastime

A winter adventure, that's truly sublime

A Canadian tradition

Ice Blade Dancing

Ice skating, a winter tradition

A glide on the ice, an admission

The crisp air, a refreshing breeze

Nature's beauty, in winter freeze

The sound of blades, cutting the ice

A feeling of freedom, a sense of entice

The cold on the cheeks, a rosy hue

A winter activity, that's utterly new

The ice so smooth, a reflection of light

A winter wonderland, so bright and white

The twirls and spins, a graceful dance

A feeling of euphoria, a romance

Ice skating, a Canadian pastime

A winter activity, that's sublime

A tradition that's passed down through the
ages

A winter sport, that engages

Ice skating, fun for all ages

John Candy

John Candy, a comedy legend

A talent that we miss

With a smile so wide, and a laugh so big

He left an impression, which was genuinely
hearty

From SCTV, to the big screen

His humor, a comedic delight

A talent so vast

A pleasure to watch

In "Uncle Buck" and "Planes, Trains, and
Automobiles"

A comedic genius, with a heart of gold

John Candy, a story that will never grow old

His legacy lives on, through his every film

A reminder of a Canadian gem

A comedy legend, which will always live on

Pinecones

Pinecones, a natural wonder

A symbol of the forest regeneration

A reminder of its beauty, natures intention

From the tall pines, they fall to the ground

A symbol of autumn, and the ever-changing
seasons

Their shape, a spiral, so unique

A reminder that nothing stays the same

A symbol of renewal, and new beginnings

Pinecones, a chance to replenish the earth

In the forest, they lay, a natural bed

A decoration, used, in so many ways

A natural wonder, so simple yet so pretty

A real beauty, eh

The Toronto Zoo

Toronto Zoo, a wild adventure

A journey through the animal kingdom

A sanctuary for the animals, exotic indeed

A place where the wildlife lives close by

The roar of the lions, heard at night

The trumpeting of the elephants, an amazing
spectacle

The chatter of the monkeys, a fun sound to
hear

The Toronto Zoo is wonderous

The exhibits, a representation worldwide

Of the animal kingdom, and its conservation

A place where the wild thrive

Toronto Zoo, an animal hive

The Toronto Zoo, another symbol of Ontario

A reminder of nature beyond our land

So why not come and explore,

the animal kingdom

A sanctuary for the beasts

A visiting pleasure

Caribana Delight

Caribana, a celebration of culture

A festival of music and dance

A display of vibrant colors, true delight

A celebration of Caribbean heritage, fantastic
food all around

The sound of steel drums

The rhythm of reggae

The beat of soca

Caribana, a true Caribbean round

The costumes, a representation

Caribbean culture, its vibrant sensation

A display of creativity, and artistic expression

The festival, a symbol of cultural diversity

Let's dance into the night

Let the Jazz Play

Jazz Festival, a celebration of sound

A symphony of notes, that never hit the ground

A melody of improvisation

A celebration of jazz music, Quebec puts on a
show

The sound of the trumpets

The rhythm of the drums

The beat of the bass

A sound of the Jazz Festival

The performers, a representation

Of jazz music and its improvisation

A display of talent, and artistic expression

Jazz Festival, a musical session

The festival we gather to listen

A celebration of sound, which will always ignite

So, enjoy, the harmony of jazz

A celebration of music

A symphony of notes

Canada's Wonderland

Canada's Wonderland, a wonder of the land

A place of excitement, adventure, and play

A theme park, that never fails to amaze

A playground of fun, which will always raise
cheer

The rollercoaster

The water rides

The attractions and novelty foods

Canada's Wonderland you got the goods

Of excitement, fun for everyone

A place of entertainment, fireworks

Canada's Wonderland, we Canadians do love

The park, a symbol of Ontario

A reminder of great childhood memories

A playground of fun

The Mighty Water Fall

Niagara Falls, a remarkable sight to behold

A natural wonder

Of the power and beauty of the water

A mesmerizing sight

Its waters glisten in the sunlight

The water rushing down from above

A thundering sound, it rings in our ears

Many have tried to conquer in barrels and contraptions

The mist rising, a peaceful sprinkle I feel on my face

The rainbow shines in the midst, a sight so grand

Niagara Falls

The water just flows, it never ever stops

A reminder of life's constant way

But the falls will forever be

Long after my children's children have grown

The lights at night reflected, they put on a show

Niagara Falls where the vine for wine grows

Muskoka Tranquility

Muskoka, a land of serenity

Nature's canvas, an artist's delight

Lakes and forests, the perfect blend

Tranquility, around every bend

The loons call out, a melody so sweet

The sunsets, casting its golden treat

Boats glide along, leaving a wake

A symphony of nature, our hearts soak it in

The rocky shores a place to contemplate

Wildlife roams, the forest's sage

The cool breeze, a refreshing kiss on the face

Muskoka, is just bliss

The night sky, northern lights display

A reminder of the beauty we often forget

Muskoka

A great place to reset

The Hill

Ottawa, city of culture and pride

Where history and progress reside

From Parliament Hill to the Rideau Canal

A glimpse of Canada's governed

The ByWard Market bustles with life

Farmers sell local produce, makes the mouth
water and the belly rumble

The National Arts Centre shines

A cultural hub in this special place

The Museum of History tells its tale,

Of Canada's past, both grand and frail

And in the wintertime, the ice shines bright,

As skaters glide along the frozen sight

Ottawa,

A city of diversity,

Where cultures come together

A reflection of Canada's heart

Where art and history meld together and play their part

Gem on the Lake

Center Island, a gem on the lake,

A peaceful retreat for all to take

Ferries cross the water with ease,

Bringing visitors to this lovely place with trees

The island's lush with greenery,

A perfect spot for a family

Bicycles for rent, trails to explore,

Nature's beauty, an open door

The beaches are fine

And as the sun sets on the horizon,

The skyline of Toronto comes into view

Center Island, a place to unwind,

Leave the hustle and bustle behind

A sanctuary in the heart of the city,

A place to find tranquility

It's a Canadian thing, eh

The Toronto Maple Leaf's, a team with ambition

With a blue and white sweater, and a "L" on the crest

The city's pride, a symbol of hope,

For a Stanley Cup, the fans wish one day again

With skates on the ice, the players glide,

The crowd roars, as they take the lead

GOAL!

The Air Canada Centre, a wave of blue and white,

The pride of Toronto

With legends like Bower and Keon,

Sundin and Tavares

The Leaf's Nation, strong,

For their team, they'll sing this song

The future's bright, in this we hold fast

The Toronto Maple Leaf's, hockey

A team of passion and Canadian pride

Forever etched in our hearts

Toronto Maple Leaf's Fan Pride

Cherry Beach Love

Cherry Beach, a hidden gem,

On the shores of Lake Ontario, a place for a walk

A place where the city comes alive,

With sun, sand, and the sound of waves thrive

The beach is a place to relax and unwind,

Where memories made

With the sun shining down, and a gentle breeze,

Cherry Beach is the place to be at ease

As the sun sets, the sky turns pink,

A sight to see

The city's skyline in the distance,

A reminder of life's persistence

Cherry Beach, a place to gather

Where Toronto's beauty can be felt

A place where the city comes together,

As one, in the warmth of summer weather

Market of Culture

Kensington Market, a neighborhood so grand,

With streets lined with shops, and food from
every land

Where cultures come together,

A melting pots

The market bustles with life and sound,

Where vendors sell their wares, all around

From fresh produce to vintage clothes,

There's always something new to try

The aroma of spices and foods,

Fills the air and sets the mood

To explore diverse cultures

Kensington Market, diversity at its finest

Where people come together

A neighborhood that's full of life,

A place where the streets are alive

With music, art, you see all around

A hidden gem in the heart of the city,

A place that's always bustling in this beautiful city

Thousand Islands of Bliss

The Thousand Islands, a sight to see,

With water as far as the eye can see.

A place of natural beauty, serene,

Where the St. Lawrence River flows

The islands, small and large,

A playground for nature's charge

From boating to fishing, swimming too,

There's something for everyone to do

The Boldt Castle

A reminder of love, once so bright

The Thousand Islands Bridge, a feat of
engineering

A link to the past, and a future worth clinging

The Thousand Islands, a place to escape

A destination to explored,

Where history and nature, seamlessly meshed

EH

We Canadians, we say "eh" here and there

It's a word that's unique, you wouldn't
understand, you must be here

We use it all the time

It's a national pastime

In every sentence, it's thrown in

Like a cherry on top, it's a win

It's a way to express surprise,

Or to emphasize, with no guise

"Nice weather, eh?" they'll say with a grin,

"That was a close call, eh?" they'll chime

"Eh" is a word of many uses,

It's a part of Canadian culture, no excuses

So, if you're ever in Canada,

Don't be shy, give "eh" a try-a.

You'll fit right in, with the locals,

And you'll be speaking Canadian like a pro

Remember also when talking not to forget

Canadians need to say sorry, eh

For all and anything really, okay

We don't know why, so just let us say it

You'll end up repeating it

I guarantee it

I don't live in an Igloo, eh!

Canadians, they don't live in igloos,

It's a stereotype that's not true

We live in houses, just like you,

With a roof and walls, and a view

Igloos made of ice, you see,

And they're not meant for you or me

They're a part of Inuit culture,

A traditional shelter

Canada is a vast country,

With diverse landscapes, it's not just snow and ice

From mountains to prairies, and forests to sea,

There's so much to explore, and so much to see

So, when you think of Canada,

Don't think of igloos, that's not the plan-a.

Think of a place of beauty and wonder

That's where you'll find us Canadians

Not buried deep in houses made of snow

The Six

The 416, a place of energy and life,

Where the streets are always alive and vibing

A city within a city, where culture abounds,

A place that's always growing, never stagnant

The 416, where the CN Tower stands tall,

A beacon of the city, visible to all

A symbol of progress and of pride,

A view from the top, that's hard to hide

The 416, where the streets are lined with art,

A place where creativity plays a special part

From graffiti to street performers, the art is
diverse,

A reflection of the city, and its people

The 416, a place where food is always fresh,

Where restaurants and food trucks, never take
a rest

A melting pot of cultures, where flavors are
diverse,

A taste of the world, for all to immerse

The 416, a city that's always on the move,

A place where dreams come true, and people groove

A place that's full of life, and energy,

A city that's always evolving, and never boring, see

The Dome of Hopes

The Sky-dome, a marvel of engineering,

A structure that's built to last

A stadium like no other, with a roof that's
unique

Sports and entertainment, a place to gather

The Sky-dome, where baseball plays,

Where the crowd cheers, and the players' skills
displayed

A place where home runs fly, and catches are
made,

A stadium that's become a part of Toronto

The Sky-dome, where concerts held,

Where music echoes for all to hear

A place where memories create

The Sky-dome, a place where history made,

Where championship games won, and records
are made

A stadium that's seen it all, from triumph to defeat,

A place that's always been at the heart of the city

The Sky-dome, a Toronto staple

A stadium that's etched in the city's history

A whale's tail, Yum

Oh, sweet and savory tail,

Fried to perfection.

A Canadian dessert that's sweet

A treat that's sure to please

With toppings of your choice to pick,

From chocolate hazelnut to maple syrup

A delicious snack that's hard to beat,

A must-try for those sweet tooths

So, if you're ever in Canada,

And looking for a snack to savor,

Try a beaver tail, moose tongue or whale tail

A tasty treat whose name is hard to forget

Soft, flaky, warm, and sweet,

A Canadian classic treat, through and through

A treat that's sure to make your day

Oh Henry, Thank you!

Fort Henry, oh grand and old,

A fortress built in days of old

A testament to Canada's past,

A history lesson that will last

With walls of stone and cannons grand,

A sight to see, a sight to stand

The fort, a symbol of our pride,

A glimpse into our nation's side

Built to protect and guard the land,

From invaders, it took a stand

A beacon of our nation's strength,

A symbol of our length

And now, the fort is open wide,

For all to take a ride

Through history

Fort Henry's stories to continue

So, see this grand old fort,

And learn about our nation's sort

A glimpse into our past,

Fort Henry, a treasure that will last

It's over eh, sorry.

Abbreviations for non-Canadians

"Hoser" is a slang word for a Canadian of limited intelligence and little education. Always a white man, a hoser is, to some extent, the Canadian equivalent of American terms like "hillbilly" and "redneck" – though without the overtly racist connotations of the latter word.

Canadians' emphasis this when subjected to other people point out where we came from and start talking to us with the, EH. Or A.

-The Canadian Encyclopedia and Lizy.

Toronto is called the 6 thanks to Forest Hill 'hood rapper Drake, who refers to his hometown as the 6 when he named his album. At one time it was called the 416 which I believe was and is much cooler. Sorry Drake.

The proper way to pronounce Toronto is as follows: Torono. The T is silent

About the Author

Lizy is a Canadian author, illustrator, and now
owner of The Elite Lizzard Publishing Company.
She has over twenty-three published books in
different genres written. She loves creating
books that help kids learn!
Find all her poetry books on Amazon, Barnes,
Noble and other online bookstores.

Are you a fan? Get updates on <u>new books!</u>
Elitelizzardpublishing@hotmail.com

*If you liked this book please leave a review.
It helps get these books seen.

www.ingramcontent.com/pod-product-compliance
Lightning Source LLC
Chambersburg PA
CBHW071517030726
47593CB00003B/1302